People in My Community

Firefighter

by Jacqueline Laks Gorman
Photographs by Gregg Andersen

Reading consultant: Susan Nations, M.Ed., author/literacy coach/consultant

WEEKLY WR READER®
EARLY LEARNING LIBRARY

Please visit our web site at: **www.earlyliteracy.cc**
For a free color catalog describing **Weekly Reader**® **Early Learning Library's**
list of high-quality books, call 1-877-445-5824 (USA) or 1-800-387-3178 (Canada).
Weekly Reader® **Early Learning Library's fax:** (414) 336-0164.

Library of Congress Cataloging-in-Publication Data

Gorman, Jacqueline Laks, 1955-
    Firefighter / by Jacqueline Laks Gorman.
      p. cm. — (People in my community)
    Summary: Simple text and photographs depict the activities of a firefighter.
    Includes bibliographical references and index.
    ISBN 0-8368-3295-7 (lib. bdg.)
    ISBN 0-8368-3302-3 (softcover)
    1. Fire extinction—Juvenile literature.   2. Fire fighters—Juvenile literature.
    [1. Fire fighters.   2. Fire extinction.   3. Occupations.]   I. Title.
    TH9148.G67   2002
    628.9'25—dc21   2002024194

This edition first published in 2002 by
Weekly Reader® **Early Learning Library**
330 West Olive Street, Suite 100
Milwaukee, WI 53212 USA

Art direction and page layout: Tammy Gruenewald
Photographer: Gregg Andersen
Editorial assistant: Diane Laska-Swanke
Production: Susan Ashley

Printed in the United States of America

1 2 3 4 5 6 7 8 9 06 05 04 03 02

Note to Educators and Parents

Reading is such an exciting adventure for young children! They are beginning to integrate their oral language skills with written language. To encourage children along the path to early literacy, books must be colorful, engaging, and interesting; they should invite the young reader to explore both the print and the pictures.

People in My Community is a new series designed to help children read about the world around them. In each book young readers will learn interesting facts about some familiar community helpers.

Each book is specially designed to support the young reader in the reading process. The familiar topics are appealing to young children and invite them to read — and re-read — again and again. The full-color photographs and enhanced text further support the student during the reading process.

In addition to serving as wonderful picture books in schools, libraries, homes, and other places where children learn to love reading, these books are specifically intended to be read within an instructional guided reading group. This small group setting allows beginning readers to work with a fluent adult model as they make meaning from the text. After children develop fluency with the text and content, the book can be read independently. Children and adults alike will find these books supportive, engaging, and fun!

— Susan Nations, M.Ed., author, literacy coach,
and consultant in literacy development

The firefighter has
an important job.
The firefighter
helps people.

Firefighters help people by protecting them from fires. They also put out fires.

Firefighters wear special helmets, coats, and boots. They wear face masks and **air tanks**, too.

air tank

9

Firefighters use special tools, like hoses, **bars**, and **axes**. They use ropes and long poles, too.

bar

ax

Firefighters ride in fire trucks. They turn on the siren and drive very fast to get to the fire.

When firefighters get to a fire, they use water and foam to put out the fire.

Firefighters use **ladders**, too. They rescue people. They give first aid to people who are hurt.

ladder

Firefighters visit schools. They tell you how to prevent fires and what to do if there is a fire.

It looks like fun
to be a firefighter.
Would you like to
be a firefighter
some day?

Glossary

air tanks — special containers that carry air so someone can breathe

axes — tools with sharp blades on one end

first aid — emergency care that is given as soon as possible to someone who is hurt or sick

foam — bubbles that are used to put out fires

For More Information

Fiction Books

Bridwell, Norman. *Clifford the Firehouse Dog.*
  New York: Scholastic, 1992.
Brown, Marc. *Arthur's Fire Drill.* New York:
  Random House, 2000.

Nonfiction Books

Klingel, Cynthia and Robert B. Noyed. *Firefighters.*
  Chanhassen, Minn.: Child's World, 2002.
Schaefer, Lola M. *We Need Fire Fighters.* Mankato,
  Minn.: Pebble Books, 2000.

Web Sites
U.S. Fire Administration's Kids Page
www.usfa.fema.gov/kids
For games and information on fire safety and how
to become a junior fire marshal

Index

About the Author

Jacqueline Laks Gorman is a writer and editor. She grew up in New York City and began her career working on encyclopedias and other reference books. Since then, she has worked on many different kinds of books. She lives with her husband and children, Colin and Caitlin, in DeKalb, Illinois.